Arthur Clark Kennedy, Maurice Greiffenhagen

Pictures In Rhyme

Arthur Clark Kennedy, Maurice Greiffenhagen

Pictures In Rhyme

ISBN/EAN: 9783337394523

Printed in Europe, USA, Canada, Australia, Japan

Cover: Foto ©Thomas Meinert / pixelio.de

More available books at **www.hansebooks.com**

PICTURES IN RHYME

BY

ARTHUR CLARK KENNEDY

ILLUSTRATED BY MAURICE GREIFFENHAGEN

LONDON
LONGMANS, GREEN, AND CO.
AND NEW YORK : 15 EAST 16th STREET
1891

CONTENTS

	PAGE
La Marquise de Pompadour (illust. Frontispiece)	1
The Witches' Warning	3
Will He Forgive?	4
Sisera	6
Upon the Sands	8
Under the Snowy Steppes	10
An Assignation	13
At Kassassin	14
Vivienique (illust.)	18
The Poet's Prophecy	19
In the Night	21
The Sale of the World	23
Death and Dives (illust.)	26
Street Music	29
Sir Alexander's Desk	31
On the Stair (illust.)	36
One Little Year To-day	40
'He was a Prince of Power and Might'	43
Lament of Boabdil	46
'In my Dreams I see a Castle'	48
The Song	50
'When Dead is Day'	52
'Young Love unfurled his Silken Sail'	54
A Queen	56
'They tell me you have Married'	57
On a Portrait of Napoleon I. by David	59
Why?	61
The Broken Glass	62
Nor is Love Sold	63
How Strange our Lives!	65
Flower of the Flowers	67
A Desert Night	69
Two Friends I knew	70
The Icicle Queen	71
Flower and Fruit	73
'Cinderella' by Millais	74
The Morning Mist	75
At Malvern Wells	76
The Summons of Spring	78
Street Arabs	79
'The Patter of Tiny Feet'	81
Illusions Perdues	82

ILLUSTRATIONS

SHE WAS MADAME DE POMPADOUR . . *Frontispiece*

OUR NOBLEST AIMS ARE WRECKED BY FINGERS FAIR,
AMBITION'S SHROUD, A WEB OF WOMAN'S HAIR . *To face page* 18

'BEHOLD! HOW MUCH I GIVE TO THEE
IN PLACE OF ALL THOU LEAV'ST FOR ME' . ,, 28

IN HIS HAND A GLITTERING RAPIER SHONE ,, 36

LA MARQUISE DE POMPADOUR

She was Madame de Pompadour,
   I wore a George's hunting-dress
When we wandered aside for a short, sweet hour,
   From the masked and whirling press.

Nooked in a cool recess we sat,
   Whilst her tongue, like a bee from flower to flower,
First touched on this, and then on that—
   Madame de Pompadour.

Many a laughing word was said
   Ere a hush crept over that green alcove,
And the light tongue ceased, for another had strayed
   Into the perilous paths of love.

At first our hands met, then our eyes,
   And then our lips. Ah! that short, sweet hour
In which I won her, my life-set prize,
   Madame de Pompadour.

Won her, and wore her a week—no more;
    But that week outweighs all years to me,
For she then was *my* Madame de Pompadour,
    As she yet again will be.

Alas! in the shade of that dim recess,
    Under the flickering Chinese lamp,
On that dainty head and powdered tress
    Other lips set their stamp.

A chill neglected. One little week,
    And beneath a ringing, indented stone
She slept, where incense and music seek
    To mingle fragrance and tone.

Ashes to ashes, dust to dust—
    Let the dead past bury its dead;
But I still hold my heart in trust,
    Unmated and unwed.

THE WITCHES' WARNING

THE earl looked seaward over his walls;
    But all he saw was a wreath of mist,
    And a little black cloud, by the white moon kissed :
So he turned again to his lighted halls.

But the wreath of mist hid an enemy's ships,
    As it slowly crept with them into the bay;
    And the little cloud rolled up, ragged and grey,
With livid lightning between its lips.

A levin-bolt split the castle keep,
    And opened a way for the enemy's sword ;
    But the Earl still smiled at the witches' word
When they killed him in his sleep.

WILL HE FORGIVE?

CLASPED in another's arms, and forced to smile—
To lip, to laugh, whilst, distant many a mile,
He lies under the sod.   O God!

My heart is buried with him; only the husk, the shell,
This man holds. And yet my mother says: 'It is well—
Thou art rich, and should'st rejoice in my choice.'

Compared with this man he was poor, though glorious of soul and face;
But a crooked back and mind are accounted small disgrace—
To have a shrunken purse is worse.

So, lapped in the splendours of state,
I live with a man that I hate—

Hating myself. Yet I live,
And wonder whether he knows
Under the sunshine and snows,
And whether he will forgive.

SISERA

Eyes seeking what the distance never brought,
Strained through a lattice-window finely wrought—
Sweet-smelling veil of woven cedar-wood.

Where the white pigeons lit, and softly cooed,
Ere fluttering down to their accustomed food
In the broad, marble, many-creviced court.

. . . . . .

The brook of Kishon slowly reddening ;
The trailing chariot, and the bitter ring
Of intercepted, swift-descending swords.

The panting fugitive. The lying words,
' Turn in ; behold this tent, it is my lord's ! '
The cloak of camel's hair for safe shrouding.

The lordly dish of butter, and the nail;
The hammer in the nervous hand of Jael;
The blow which crashed through temple and through
    brain.

A sheet of summer lightning, and red rain
Across the sleeper's sight. A sense of pain
But scarce begun ere sense and senses fail.

The sand-fed sun, low-lying on the lands;
The tent door curtained where a woman stands,
And the unspoken: 'This is whom you seek.'

The song of praise: 'The battle to the weak.
Praise ye the Lord, who hath upheld the meek.
The Lord who stayeth Israel in His hands.'

UPON THE SANDS

I TOOK his cheeks between my hands,
    I kissed his face and forehead o'er,
Where he lay on the sheeted sands
    Which stretched along the shore.

The surf crawled slowly up, and sad,
    Like some sea-dog which owned his sway,
And yet had rent him—sightless, mad,
    It came and moaned all day.

But there he lay, so still and white;
    I dared not weep, I thought he slept.
The tearless day shrank back from night;
    I might have woke him had I wept.

The night sank down into the seas,
    New morning burst upon the skies;
And with its first breath on the breeze
    I stooped and kissed his eyes.

But when he woke not even then,
  Although my whispers stirred his hair,
I knew he breathed, away from men,
  A higher and a purer air.

The essence of a Godhead's breath,
  And that the sleep my darling slept,
Was called of us the body's death—
  And then at length I wept.

UNDER THE SNOWY STEPPES

She ruled a wide domain; and he
Her steward's son, but just set free
On life, and breathing of passion ever,
Till under the snowy steppes, adown the silent river,
Where the dark pines gather, where their dark plumes
    quiver,
He found a sepulchre.

She loved, and let her fancy range;
Such woman's love—the love of change,
Tired ere well begun, and constant never.
Under the snowy steppes, down the silent river,
Where the dark pines gather, where their dark plumes
    quiver,
Is a sepulchre.

She gazed upon that boyish face,
Ensnared him with voluptuous grace,
Bound body and soul her prisoner.

Under the snowy steppes, down the silent river,
Where the dark pines gather, where their dark plumes
    quiver,
Is his sepulchre.

Her woven meshes interlaced
His being; clasped, in sin embraced,
He yielded him, willing idolater.
Under the snowy steppes, down the silent river,
Where the dark pines gather, where their dark plumes
    quiver,
Is his sepulchre.

Her love burnt bright till, gorged, o'er-fed—
Love born of lust is soonest dead!—
To loose his bonds was her endeavour.
Under the snowy steppes, down the silent river,
Where the dark pines gather, where their dark plumes
    quiver,
Is his sepulchre.

His love consumed his inmost soul,
Resistless, passed beyond control;
From his love with life he could not sever.

Under the snowy steppes, down the silent river,
Where the dark pines gather, where their dark plumes
    quiver,
Is his sepulchre.

He urged his love with passionate force ;
She offered gold, and said, 'One course
Is open : depart, and see me never.'
Under the snowy steppes, down the silent river,
Where the dark pines gather, where their dark plumes
    quiver,
Is his sepulchre.

Then laughed. That laugh, hell-echoed, stirred
His bosom's core. She pass'd. He heard
That laugh ring on in his ears for ever ;
Till under the snowy steppes, adown the silent river,
Where the dark pines gather, where their dark plumes
    quiver,
He found a sepulchre.

AN ASSIGNATION

A LADDER hung snake-like and limp to the breeze;
A figure which steals through the shadow-clad trees,
And sways up the knotted stair;
An open casement which welcomes the air
Of the heavy-browed night; and stranger where
A crescent-cupped light but reveals the gloom
Of four dark corners about the room.

Two steps lead to the lady's bed—
Arras and cloth of red.

Bending to wake her with love's caresses,
He slips one arm 'neath her rich brown tresses,
And whispers words she can never hear,
For her throat is cut from ear to ear.

AT KASSASSIN

Rained on all day by the sun,
Beating through helmet and head,
Through to the brain.
Inactive, no water, no bread,
We had stood on the desolate plain
Till evening shades drew on amain ;
And we thought that our day's work was done,
When, lo! it had only begun.

'Charge!' And away through the night,
Toward the red flashes of light
Spurting in fire on our sight,
Swifter and swifter we sped.
'Charge!' At that word of command,
On through the loose-holding sand,
On through the hot, folding sand,
Through hailstorms of iron and lead,
Swifter and swifter we sped.

Thud! fell a friend at my hand;
No halt, ne'er a stay, nor a stand.
What though a comrade fell dead?
Swifter and swifter we sped.

Only the red, flashing light
Guided our purpose aright;
For night was upon us, around,
Deceptive in sight as in sound.
We knew not the enemy's ground,
We knew not his force;
But on, gaining pace at each bound,
Flew man and horse.

Burst on the enemy's flank,
On through his gunners and guns,
Swifter and swifter we sped;
Over each bayonet-ranged rank,
Earthward their dusky waves sank,
Scattered and fled.

They ran as a startled flock runs ;
But still we pursued o'er the plain,
Till the rising moon counted the slain,
And some hundred Egyptians lay dead.

Oh ! 'twas a glorious ride,
And I rode on the crest of the tide.
We dashed them aside like the mud of the street,
We threshed them away like the chaff from the wheat,
We trod out their victory under our feet,
And charged them again and again ;
For demons were loose on the hot-breathing wind,
And entered the souls of our men.
A feverish delight filled our bones,
Heightened by curses and groans—
The mind taking hold of the body, the body reacting on mind.

Ha ! 'twas a glorious ride,
Though I miss an old friend from my side,

And sadness is mingled with pride.
Still, 'twas a glorious ride—
That race through the darkness, the straining, the shock,
The struggle, and slaughter by Kassassin lock.

VIVIENIQUE

Man's aspirations oft are drown'd in eyes—
Twin wells, their depth as fathomless as full;
Whiles ofttime Honour, lured by woman's sighs—
Bound, fettered fast beneath a woman's rule—
Has from Life's ploughshare turned himself aback,
Mock'd, helpless, down along the limèd track,.
To breathe his soul out in soft vestibule,
Afar from tented field and council-board.
Folly and sin entail their own reward:
Our noblest aims are wrecked by fingers fair,
Ambition's shroud, a web of woman's hair.

THE POET'S PROPHECY

He walked through the midst of the crowd
    A mark for each scornful eye,
But lifted his gaze to a golden cloud
    At anchorage in the sky,
And smiled, as he murmured, half-aloud:
    'I shall live when all these die.

'That fair dame's beauty shall fade—
    Food for worms to batten upon;
Yon warrior's laurels within the shade
    Grow withered, sere, and brown;
The price of that prelate's pride be paid
    With an effigy in stone.'

The golden cloud sailed into the West,
    Where the sun in blood sank down;

While the poet passed to his humble nest
   By the river-ways of town.
'Tis years since then, and, called from their rest,
The crowd would find that the poet knew best—
   He lives in his renown.

IN THE NIGHT

CHALK cliffs a thousand feet in height,
Grey ghosts melting into the night.

And on their summit, to and fro,
Doomed on his weary beat to go,
Every night from ten till two,
A Coastguard paces to and fro.
If the wind blows high, if the wind blows low,
Through the pelting rain, through the driving
    snow,
To and fro, to and fro.

On the look-out lest a wrecker's light
    Over the lower downs should glide,
Swung from a horse, whose motions might
    Show like a boat on the heaving tide,
Luring rich ships, by its baleful glare,
Into that horrible, hidden snare;

From whose maw agape, with rock-set teeth,
Every breath seems charged with death.

To guide his feet a line is laid
Of chalk-blocks, whiter with whitewash made,
   Over the green, elastic turf;
And his perch is so high that he cannot hear,
Even with his accustomed ear,
   The monotonous-sounding swish of the surf.

      To-night there's a fight
'Twixt the god of the sea and the gods of the air,
And there's death and destruction afloat everywhere.

The flaps of his oilskin like whipthongs crack,
As the Coastguard seeks his wonted track.

But the line leads over the cliff's pent brow,
And he falls a thousand feet below.

His cry, caught up by the rush of the air,
Startles the guillemots' nestless lair.

Who was it said, 'A life for a life'?—
And a smuggler marries the widowed wife.

THE SALE OF THE WORLD

THE world, the fair world, with her bosoms of snow,
Her life-pulses bounding in turbulent flow,
Lies prone in the scale,
Exposed and for sale;
Save for forests of hair
From her temples down-curled,
Exposed to a critical, insolent stare.
Who will buy? Who will bid? Who will weigh up
 the world?

Who will buy? Who will bid? Who will weigh up
 the world?
—'Mid the blare of curved trumpets, with banners
 unfurled,
A Genius takes form
From the breath of the storm—
Tall and gaunt,
Scarred of front;

Blown over a blood-bestained vest,
A tawny beard, sweeping his chest,
Reaches down to the clasp of his girth.
At his footsteps the earth
Shrinks back in affright;
Cloud-vultures of night
Flap their pestilent pinions in flight
Closely after.

A blue gleam, then a clang:
Whence the shaking scales hang,
As shield follows helmet, and helmet the brand,
Backpiece, breastplate, and greaves;
Last, the mighty spear leaves
His knotted right hand—
But the scale only quivers up under the rafter.

As day dissolves night when it steals up the sky,
As night disappears in the distance to die,
See a form in bright garments approach like a ray
Falling down from the sun, and war-clouds melt away:
Broad brow; scanty locks o'er a thin, pallid face;
Eyes lit with deep eagerness, beaming with grace

From a strong-seated learning. The shoulders' slight
    stoop,
Bowed down by the spirits which burden the croup
Of his mule in their casings, stiff wood-ribs and hide.
The weight of his intellect, learning, and looks,
His scrolls and his parchments, his papers and books,
He casts in the scale, then himself climbs inside—
But all weigh as nothing, discounted of worth
Against the full nature and grossness of earth.

A smoky glare
Of torches, which jaundice the lower air,
And blacken the forehead of Heaven,
As the children of Mammon toil up to the scale,
Seven times seventy-seven.
In they pour their glittering store,
Stream on stream,
Till the scale with the world flashes up to the beam,
Bought and sold—
Sold to the sons of the Genius of Gold.
Thus the fair Universe,
Untouched by the power of the sword,
Unmoved by the power of the word,
Is enthralled by the power of the purse.

DEATH AND DIVES

DEATH

' RISE up, rise up, put off those robes,
   And follow me into the night;
Leave thy gay feast, thy glittering globes;
   Let fall the scales which mar thy sight;
Throw thy half-tasted winecup down—
   Thou hast a deeper draught to drink
When wrapped within my sable gown,
   Forgetting self, forget to think.
Obey, obey!
   I have no time to pause, to stay;
   We must be far away
Ere day.'

DIVES

' What! go with thee, thou fearful guest;
Be wrapped upon thy fatal breast,
   To sleep forgetting and forgot?
Leave this my home of life and light,
To pass with thee across the night,
   Unknown? I will not.'

DEATH

'Obey, obey!
  I have no time to pause, to stay;
  We must be far away
Ere day.'

DIVES

' I scarcely yet begin to live
  After the years of gathering toil,
Needing no longer now to strive,
  My cellars filled with wine and oil.
My honey-bees do congregate
Near barns which groan beneath the weight
Of corn, and shrivelled fruit, in rows,
Hangs rafter-strung; whilst daily grows
More loud the lowing in my stalls.
Atlanta, too, this day has foaled.
These jars of silver, bowls of gold,
These purple robes of sea-born dye,
Yon gaudy birds which swing and cry
In unknown, brazen tongues. Yon slaves,
  Spice-scented, from whose viols falls
  Soft music on my painted walls,
Passion and sleep's melodious waves.

Through heat, through cold, o'er distant seas,
Now fanned, now baffled by the breeze,
I gathered these.
And then thou askest me,
Leaving my glittering halls, to pass with thee
From men, from light,
Into the voiceless night.'

Death smiled upon him, and then said,
As his lips gently touched his head :
' Behold ! how much I give to thee
In place of all thou leav'st for me.'

Thou gav'st them, through cold'st of a distant isle,
Sigw'd around, now hush'd by the breeze.
I gathered them,
And then thou makest me,
Leaving my glittering halls, to pass with thee
From sun from light
Into this rainless night.'

Death smiled upon him, and then said,
As his lips gently touched in hand:
'Behold! how much · give to thee
In place of all thou sav'st for me.'

*Behold: how much I give to thee
In place of all thou leav'st for me*

STREET MUSIC

THE city's labour, in lumbering throes,
   On the other side of my garden-wall,
Like the pant of an engine, fell and rose;
And my mind ran faster than facile pen
Could follow it over the paper, when
I suddenly heard an old, old tune,
And lived again in that month of June,
    And again I saw it all.

My nostrils greeted the scent of the hay
   In fields where the pollards drew down rain,
Where low in the hollow the cattle lay
Chewing the cud, and flicking the flies,
With lazy content in their dreamy eyes,
    Unstreaked by thoughtful pain.

The white-walled cottage with moss-grown thatch,
   The thin spire peering above the hill,

Under the coppice a clover-patch,
A swinging gate, and a sun-kiss'd maid ;
And I heard once more what those sweet lips said ;
   And those sweet lips said : ' I will.'

Her hair fell rippling over her neck,
   Her face a-blush like a budding rose,
So soft, so pure, with never a speck.
Ah ! who would have thought of the scatter'd leaves,
And the aphis at heart ! How the face deceives,
   Though blind Love thinks he knows !

Then my lips were parched with a longing thirst,
And my temples throbbed as though they would burst,
Till the tune died away, and another ran
From under the hand of the organ-man :
And June was not, but November drear,
Wearing her weeds for the dying year.

SIR ALEXANDER'S DESK

IN the wan shadow-land which lies
Hidden from sight of human eyes,
  Half-way 'twixt here and Heaven,
You, my good grandfather, await
The utterance of that mandate
  Which strikes all odd scores even.

I, still on earth, am curious
To know, could you but tell it us,
  The whole veracious story
Of this, your dead and done romance,
When Bonapartè ruled in France,
  And you won glory.

A case of coromandel wood,
Brass-bound, shield-locked, which I found stood
  Aside in our old store-room,
Never unlocked since that day when,

Some nearly threescore years and ten,
   In times of doubt and war-gloom,

You fastened it yourself with care—
A shrine which held two hearts laid bare—
   And thus inscribed the packet:
'If I should fall, as fall I may,
Bury this in my grave, I pray;'
   Then donned your martial jacket,

And galloped off to face the foe
Upon the field of Waterloo,
   Where, one long June day,
Cannon and musket, sword and lance,
Did, in our hands, for men of France
   A lively tune play.

And in that dance of fiery sounds
You lost two horses, gained two wounds,
   A flag, some female pity
From her who nursed you, brought you round,
Though doctors doomed you to the ground
   In Belgic city.

I forced the case, and peered within—
It seemed like sacrilege to win
　Your secrets dust-encrusted.
Then I undid, with reverent hands,
A parcel from its swathing-bands
　Of ribbon, rusted.

From the split, yellow folds there fell
An agate seal—a rose as well,
　Half-dust, half-wilted ;
Some letters writ on paper thin ;
Then, last, a miniature within
　A sachet, quilted.

Painted by hand of Cosway, too !
A gracious lady, robed in blue,
　Dark-eyed, with ringlets raven,
In a broad rim of garnets set ;
' S. C.,' beneath a coronet,
　At back engraven.

Who was the dainty dame ? Is this
A record of forbidden bliss ?
　Was she another's ?

Was she———? But this at least I know,
That face portrayed in smiling show
   Was *not* grandmother's!

Did she die early? Or did Fate
And cruel parents dissipate
   Your rapturous dreaming,
And make you picture Gretna-ways—
A white face in a flying chaise,
   With dark eyes streaming?

Or did the 'fair deceitful she'
But add you to her list to be
   One amid many?
Or did she love you as you her?—
This last the theory I prefer
   Better than any.

A case of true love's crooked course:
Two wedded souls; a stern divorce;
   Hopes crushed, affections blighted!
Perhaps 'twas so—who knows? And yet,
Perhaps it was that coronet;
   You were but knighted!

Well, rest in peace; I'll not presume
Further to penetrate the gloom—
  Be this an ending.
See, I place all upon the fire,
Your secrets, from a funeral pyre,
  In smoke ascending.

ON THE STAIR

PARIS, 1789

In his hand a glittering rapier [1] shone,
As he stood on the stairway's topmost stone,
And quietly leaned on the balustrade,
Whilst the rabble paused, surprised, afraid
Of some treacherous ambuscade.
   But there was none,
   For he stood alone.

They had slain the guards, and broken in;
The corridors echoed their blasphemous din;
They had thrust their pikes through the panelled walls,
Their sabots clattered across the halls.
   But under the carven balustrade
   They paused, surprised, afraid.

[1] Its delicate blade called colichenade
From that Swedish spark, Count Königsmarke.

ON THE STAIR

In his hand a gleaming rapier ...
As he stood at the mirror, ... alone.
And quietly leaned on the ...
Whilst the rabble passed ... ...
Of some tremendous ev... ...
  But there was none
  For he stood alone

They had torn ... ..., and broken in;
The corridor... ... their blasphemous din;
They had ... ... pikes through the panelled
    walls.
There was ... ... scattered across the halls.
    ... ... the seven tabernacle
        ... surprised, afraid
            ... ...
            ... ...

"In his hand a glittering rapier shone"

A vase of bronze was held in its place,
On the stair-angle's marble face,
   By its Bacchanalian handle ;
And golden lilies were growing therein,
Type of the great who ne'er toil or spin ;
   And each lily held a candle.

Whilst the late Court painter's Nymph-ideal,
   Devoid of expression or feeling,
Balanced upon an impossible heel,
   Smiled vacantly down from the ceiling.

At last a murmur from low to loud,
Rustled and swelled across the crowd,
   Which stood at bay
   On the main stairway.

And Jean the butcher lifted his axe
To split that brow 'neath its curls of flax,
   And cure its brains of their rambles ;
But there was a sudden, steely flash,
And Jean the butcher fell with a crash,
   Like an ox of his own in the shambles,

Then Bras-de-fer and porter Pierre,
And José, the Spanish commissionaire,
   Pressed up the polished stair.

The smith went down with a ball in his brain;
And, sheathed in the swarthy son of Spain,
   The rapier snapped at its silver hilt;
Whilst Pierre dropped dead without a groan,
   For the vase, with its lilies candled and gilt,
Lit on and splintered his frontal bone:
   And the crowd once more recoiled, dismayed,
   From that marble balustrade
Where he stood unarmed, alone.

He glanced at the clock above the stair:—
   He had gained her time to fly;
His lips moved once with a silent prayer,
   As he stood there to die.

Three pikes pierced his 'broidered vest,
And, clashing, met in his breast.

Little she recked that his life-blood flowed—
She had saved her jewel-case from the crowd!

They tore the buckles out of his shoes,
    The diamond rings from his finger,
Then trampled across him—no time to lose
    Nor linger.
But a ray of sunlight stole up the stair,
And dropped an aureole over his hair.

   .   .   .   .   .   .

The place where the palace stood you scan
    In vain, for the palace no longer is there :
    Not a stone is left of that marble stair,
And the clock is sold to a nobleman
    For his château in Angleterre.

Whilst Boucher's Nymph, so rosy of hue,
Twirling her scarf of vaporous blue,
Still smiles—in New York's Fifth Avenue.

ONE LITTLE YEAR TO-DAY

One year since we were married, three thousand
    miles away ;
It seems so long, sweetheart, and yet—one little year
    to-day !

It seems as if I'd known you, loved you, held you all
    my life ;
And yet—one little year to-day since first I called
    you wife !

I think we must have lived and loved in some for-
    gotten past,
In other forms, as birds or flowers, our earthy essence
    cast ;

As silver birds, in shady groves, have kissed and
    cooed and kissed,
In times agone, until our souls sank back into the
    mist.

Perchance by hand of silence sown, slept the sweet sleep of flowers,
Two blossoms borne upon one bush, in some primæval bowers.

You may have come to cradle-land in many sudden gleams,
Crept through the curtains of the night, and mingled with my dreams.

As man and woman here to-day, we breathe again in song,
Whilst the swart poppé sways our boat in solemn state along,

Beside the sea-washed, lichened walls which guard the Lido land,
Whose further, fairer side, unbound, shelves down in ribs of sand.

Skirting Venezia's arsenal, heart of her ancient might,
Which beats so slowly, faintly, now, we pass out to the right.

The haze hangs on Murano—smoke from her factory
    fires,
Where, fashioned out of rainbow hues, on hollow iron
    wires,

The glass so fair, so fragile, which the skilful work-
    men make,
Spun shapely by a single breath, another breath will
    break.

The sun behind its prison-bars sinks down into the
    flood,
Dyeing the city's watery ways with its expiring
    blood.

When we shall cease in human guise to haunt this
    world of men,
Is that the end? or will our souls revive to live again

In some state, higher, purer far than any we have
    known,
With endless life and endless love, when both shall
    be our own?

'HE WAS A PRINCE OF POWER AND MIGHT'

HE was a prince of power and might
But yesternight;
To-day
A senseless lump of coffined clay,
To hide away.

His life was one long holiday,
Careless of sorrows;
A ceaseless whirligig of play—
No thought for morrows.

His talents slept,
Securely hid,
'Neath social custom's ponderous lid;
And all men kept
The vast white pearls
Of truth from him,

Who held his wealth in changing curls
Of many girls,
By passion's passing whim.

Dusting his eyes
With flatteries,
His clouded vision
Saw fields Elysian
In scenes of rank debaucheries;
Until his name,
Of lofty fame,
Sank into shame.

He once was heard to say:
'Which is the God,
Jesus or Bacchus,
Over us?
Which heaven's true way—
Where the snow on the mountain shines,
Or where the valley's vines
Beckon and nod,
With countless clusters
Of purple lustres,

In serried line on lines,
Through smiling vale or over mountain snows?'
—But now he knows.

He was a prince of power and might
But yesternight;
To-day
A senseless lump of coffined clay,
To hide away.

LAMENT OF BOABDIL

FAIR city of waters, and thus must I leave thee?
    Thou once wast the pride of the faithful on earth:
From mine arms the mail-grasp of the Christian doth
        reve thee;
    Ah! would I had died in thee, land of my birth!

'Twere better by far that in one common downfall,
    O'erwhelmed, we had perish'd, Granada, than thou
Should'st linger in beauty, priest-govern'd, a thrall,
    A jewel in the crown on King Ferdinand's brow.

Ayesha, my mother, thou need'st not remind me
    Of all the fair realm I for ever have lost;
The Vega smiles mockingly, stretch'd far behind me,
    Bestrewn with the tents of the Cross-serving host.

O mother, my mother, now cease to upbraid me,
    Though womanly tears for an instant should flow!
Forget and forgive if my weakness betray'd me—
    My chill heart is failing like sun-melted snow.

All hopeless my future; how can I sustain it,
  For ever, Granada, an exile from thee?
If weeping comes o'er me, why should I restrain it?
  A king's tears fall not for the lands of the free.

As wending my weary way over the mountains,
  I turn me to take a last look at thy towers;
Farewell to thee ever, thou City of Fountains,
  The flag of the Christian waves over my bowers!

'IN MY DREAMS I SEE A CASTLE'

IN my dreams I see a castle standing by the Northern seas,
Where the long Atlantic rollers lash the rugged Orcades,
And a stately lady walking up and down beneath the trees.

Why does the lady wander there, in robes of white array'd?
Why does she carry in her hand a sharp and shining blade,
While her features work with agony, her eyes with fear dismay'd?

She slowly passes through the grove of wind-swept melody,
Till she stands beside the ocean, and then, full suddenly,
She cuts her heart from out her breast, and casts it in the sea.

' O western wind ! O wandering wave ! seek Southern summer seas,
Bear him my bleeding heart from these far Northern castle-leas,
And tell him I love him now much better than all these.'

But the heart was passion-weighted—passion still unpurged of pride—
On the bosom of the billows it could not safely ride ;
It never reach'd those summer seas, but sank beneath the tide.

The lady wanders still beside the dreary Northern sea,
And cries unto the wind and waves : ' Give back my heart to me.'
But the wind and waves make answer : ' That can never, never be.'

THE SONG

A MARVELLOUS voice rang, clear and sweet, through the changes of a song,
Rising and falling—to rise at the last in a tone of triumph strong:
It spoke of life, it spoke of death, of love, and of love's home,
And the soul of the singer thrill'd the crowd, and soar'd through the gilded dome.

Now the voice is dumb, and its echoes lost on the waves of infinite space,
While long, lithe grasses shake in the wind o'er the singer's sleeping-place.

The art of the singer is dead and done,
And the singer herself has gone;
   The gilded dome has sunk in decay,
   And none of that crowd survives to-day—
The song lives on alone.

And he who wrote that wondrous song—
  Did it bring him wealth and fame?
He breathed but in his song to us,
  For no one knows his name.

'WHEN DEAD IS DAY'

I LOVE the quiet night, when earth,
Shackled in iron chains of sleep,
Scarce draws her respirations deep ;
   For then I weigh
Just what this world is worth,
   When dead is day.

It is not in the night alone,
And darkness, evil things have power :
Their foreheads greet the noonday hour
   With brazen face,
Vice flaunts it on a throne
   I' the market-place.

Undeafened by humanity's low bass,
I hear the music of the spheres
Too high attuned for mortal ears
   To e'er perceive
Without night's listening-space,
   And I believe.

For revelations come when darkness falls:
'Tis then I feel an echo in my heart
Throb with a voice—that voice which says, ' Thou art,
   Though something, nothing,
And within my halls
   Subject, yet king.'

O Immortality! from mortals hid,
Is what thou art, and what thou hast in store,
When we set foot upon that further shore.
   Grasp we 'forever,'
Or is, beneath the coffin-lid,
   ' Forever, never '?

'YOUNG LOVE UNFURLED HIS SILKEN SAIL

YOUNG love unfurled his silken sail,
And in his boat of ivory pale
   Went sliding down the weather,
By sunny shores of golden isles,
Their hills o'ertopped for miles on miles
   With ruddy helms of heather.

Over seas to a shady bay,
Where, lotus-locked, enchanted lay
   He and his boat together,
Unwotting of the days that flew
In one long monotone of blue,
   From waning summer's tether.

Till heaven darkened, and the rain,
Smoking athwart the watery plain,
   Fell down with wintry weather;

Then, like a lark that upward flies,
Love swiftly lessened through the skies,
  On winnowing feather.

But the poor boat drifts on, resigned
To furies of the wave and wind,
  And wintry weather.

A QUEEN

A QUEEN—he loved her;
His queen—he moved her—
   For she was human.

Ermine robes, jewelled crown,
Thrust aside, thrown down,
   Left but a woman.

And did they blame her?
Or could it shame her?
   No! love became her.

'THEY TELL ME YOU HAVE MARRIED'

They tell me you have married
  Since I have been away;
But I, where have I tarried
  So long? you say.

A year ago I named you
  As mine; you vowed to stay
Mine only till I claimed you—
  A year to-day!

And do I find you altered?
  Your face is still the same;
But those full lips, which faltered
  Once my name,

Are pledged unto another's
  (Red wine—a goblet old);
And he has filled your mother's
  Hands with gold.

But have you quite forgotten
    Those songs we used to sing
In that dim room—begotten
    When love was king?

Why should those days return not?
    You ask me: ask that ring.
Fires of pure poesy burn not
    Where Wealth is king.

ON A PORTRAIT OF NAPOLEON I. BY DAVID

A METEOR-MAN of destiny,
Who trod,
Through others' weakness, up the paths of
 strength,
Uncumbered and unshod
Of charity,
Till in the sky
He flamed, at length,
A mid-day sun,
A people's god—
Napoleon.

His courtiers shone
Like bees upon his mantle strewn;
And yet his fate
Left him with rent robes, desolate.

ON A PORTRAIT OF NAPOLEON I. BY DAVID

How less than little was he on his throne!
How little also in his fallen days!
Whose harp can praise
Napoleon?

WHY?

EAST winds, allying
With autumn austere,
Drive beauty, dying,
Into the mere.

Under the shrill blasts
Chilling the warm blood,
A woman with wrinkles,
Back-bent and doubled,
Is gathering firewood,
Her limbs palsy-troubled.

Woman with wrinkles,
Why art thou here,
And beauty lying
Drowned in the mere?

THE BROKEN GLASS

A SUDDEN crash! A glass upon the floor,
Shatter'd in myriad pieces. A white face
Turned by a little maid toward the door,
Expectant of shrill reprimand—nay, more.
Ah! little maid, 'tis well if future store,
When Time hath furnish'd thee with fuller grace,
Shall not so shatter some fair glass of thine—
Illusion, bubble-blown, of hues divine.

NOR IS LOVE SOLD

'You've bought me with your gold,' she said,
'You've bought me with your gold;
Upon this breast you lay your head;
I would this breast were cold,' she said;
'I would this breast were cold
In churchyard mould.'

'But O! I love him well,' she said,
'But O! I love him well—
So well I would that I were dead,
And laid in narrow cell,' she said;
'And laid in narrow cell,
For life is hell.'

'Bodies are bought for gold,' she said,
'Bodies are bought for gold;

But hearts can not be forced to wed,
Though worlds grow grey and old,' she said ;
' Though worlds grow grey and old—
Nor is love sold.'

HOW STRANGE OUR LIVES!

How strange our lives! A wayward breath
   Upon the current of the mind
   May change its course—an idle wind,
Filled full with fate, or life, or death.

It comes upon us unaware,
   It steals into our very soul,
   Transmutes our being, and the whole
'What might have been' dissolves in air—

And 'That which must be' takes its place
   At some strange crisis of our life ;
   A winning or a losing strife—
Victor or vanquished in the race.

'Tis pitiful how slight a thing,
   Unsought, unnoticed at the time,
   May plunge us in a slough of crime,
Or set a bare tree blossoming.

So mean the cause, the effect so great:—
   Some single word, some simple deed,
   Which at the time we scarcely heed,
Opens the door, or shuts the gate

On our high hopes. We wander far,
   Down loveless vistas, or with Love,
   Dreaming we lie within the grove.
How few, alas! who gain that star

Which shines on each one from his birth,
   Lit with strange meanings, mystical,
   Pointed with lurid fires which shall
Mislead or guide us upon earth;

Until we win that far-off heaven,
   Across the cold, blue, glacier-steep.
   How few, alas! their foothold keep,
And to how few Faith's wings are given.

FLOWER OF THE FLOWERS

A ROSE for each year—all white, none red ;
Only white roses rest with this dead.
See how they cluster and cling round her head—
Thirty and three.
A rose in the coffin, a stroke on the bell,
Till thirty and three, three and thirty they tell—
Roses and bell.

Pick up yon rose—the one bud that has strayed—
Cast down the lid.   Our last tribute is paid
To the infant, the child, the girl, and the maid,
Wife and mother.
Let her sleep in the bloom
Of the roses' perfume,
One flower with another.
All white, white, white,
Let them sleep through the night,
To the light.

From the earth was their birth;
On the earth grew they in beauty, burning
With whitest, purest flames,
To earth returning.
Then on the coffin-lid,
Neath which the sweet, still corpse of former happy
    hours,
Till morning lieth hid,
Write we her name of names:
' Flower of the flowers!'

A DESERT NIGHT

Awake! Awake! Awake!
Stand to your arms like men;
For the muffled tread of ten thousand feet,
The roll of wheels, and redoubled beat
Of changing hoofs, are abroad on the night.
Awake!
Hark! how it comes again.
The keen night-air whispers light,
'Awake!'

. . . .

Asleep! Asleep! Asleep!
Deaf and dumb to the sounds of life,
Sand in his eyes and mouth and ears,
But awake to the secret of manifold years,
Under the broad desert-sheet he lies
Asleep!
Lost are all sounds of strife,
Dead as the body that dies.
We weep!

TWO FRIENDS I KNEW

Two men I knew—two friends, who sought a treasure :
One was a scholar, one pursued his pleasure.

Both found, or thought they found, that which they
    sought ;
In neither instance was their treasure bought.

The scholar wore his gem in all men's sight,
Pleased it should glitter, glorying in its light.

The man of social pleasures kept his close,
And strictly guarded it within his house.

The scholar's wife shines on him night and day ;
The other broke her bonds and fled away.

THE ICICLE QUEEN

TALL and stately, cold and fair,
She sits enthroned on an ivory chair,
And the sunlight is crisp in her yellow hair.

Cold, cold—so cold, in her haughty mien,
Men call her the 'Icicle Queen.'

They say she's no heart, or, if she has one,
'Tis made from a block of marble stone.

But I know there's a heart 'neath her stiff brocade—
A heart for home use, not a heart for parade.

Look close, look close; I can see it beat
And throb 'gainst her busk;
Whilst, sweet as musk,
Is the tremulous breath she draws between
Her pearly teeth, save by me unseen,
And her cheeks are flushed, but not with the heat

Love is called blind, and I love her—I!
But my eyesight is sharpened by jealousy.

Lovers come wooing this Northern Queen;
I have watched them come, I have watched them go,
Seven long years, through heat, through snow,
But I never saw yet what to-day I have seen.
Nay, 'twas not the ball-lights' fitful glow
That dazzled my sight—I saw aright
That flush in a moment come and go.

I am only her fool, misshapen, thin,
Sour, and old; I caper and grin,
My back is humpbowed, but my mind is keen,
And I sharpen my wit on the courtier-crowd.
They laugh; but she only smiles—does my queen.

. . . . . .

Ah! the closest wards own a master-key,
And *he* is to bear her across the sea;
Whilst I, her fool, must be laid on the shelf,
For she wears my motley now herself—
Ha! ha! ha! ha! does the Icicle Queen.

FLOWER AND FRUIT

THREE blossoms hung on a tree,
Three berries ripe in the sun :
One falls to the earth ; one is plucked away ;
One withers upon its stone.

Three maidens fair to see,
Three womanhoods scarce begun :
One is claimed by Death ; one marries away ;
One eats out her heart alone.

'CINDERELLA,' BY MILLAIS

FAIR Cinderella, in a pensive mood,
Kirtled in hodden-grey, and broom in hand,
Seems trembling on that mystic borderland—
That narrow strip entrenched 'twixt womanhood
And childish ways! Perplexing thoughts intrude
Upon her brain. Her Prince, though near, doth stand
As yet unseen; not yet the fairy wand
Hath changed uncertainty to certitude.
Deep, earnest eyes of wondering purity;
Vision of ruddy lips, and golden hair
Crowned with red cap of Liberty! Take care
How you exchange your maiden surety
For the full cup of love's maturity,
Lest you become less happy than you are!

THE MORNING MIST

A MIST from the channel stole up the shore,
And crept o'er the sands to a cottage-door—
Through the door, half-opened, it entered in.

A woman, ragged, haggard, and wild,
Bent a tear-stained face on her sleeping child,
Fondling its fingers pallid and thin.

But lo! before her, the morning mist
Stooped softly down with its lips, and kissed
The babe in the cradle sleeping;

Then wrapped the child on its wreathèd arm,
And melted away in the sunlight warm;
Whilst the sun dried the mother's weeping.

AT MALVERN WELLS

At Malvern Wells I ventured out:
The wind was east, but veered about
   To Nor'-nor'-east. I felt it chilly;
   My doctor called me—more than silly,
And said I well deserved the gout.

His sage advice I deigned to flout;
This was the reason why, no doubt,
I found the roads so very hilly
   At Malvern Wells.

Dull aches, rheumatic demons stout,
I strove in vain to put to rout:
   The east wind whistled very shrilly,
   Till suddenly I came on Lily
   At Malvern Wells.

I came on Lily, clad in fur;
She brought a genial warmth with her,
Diffused a glow through all my frame.
Avaunt, ye fiends! at Lilian's name,
Of health a very harbinger.

My doctor says I would aver
That she was Mercy's minister.
He says 'The Wells,' but I exclaim,
   'I came on Lily.'

Despite M.D.'s, I do not err,
Love is a potent sorcerer.
My fiends all shrank, aghast and tame,
As, no more crippled, halt, or maim,
   I came on Lily.

THE SUMMONS OF SPRING

Gallows that beckon and grin and nod,
And a strong man shrill in his agony:
'The green leaves. See, O mother of God!
The green leaves call me; I cannot die.'

His fingers grip the bars of his cell,
And his thirsty face is turned to the sky,
While his voice comes over the tolling bell:
'The green leaves call me; I cannot die.'

He is dragged down the corridors white and wide,
He is held upright 'neath the hempen ring;
But he heeds not the earnest priest at his side,
For his ears are filled with the summons of Spring.

Then this world slips from under his feet,
And he goes to that other world unshriven,
Where, I trust, when his sins are purged, he may meet
With a fairer Spring in heaven.

STREET ARABS

CHATTERING sparrows of London town,
Tailless, perky, ragged, and brown,
With a halo of smoke around you thrown.

Up on the housetops, over the slates,
Hopping about with the quaintest of gaits,
Each one abusing, ill-using his mates.

Golden canaries in vain peep through
Golden bars. Sage birds in blue,
Chained to their perches, envy you.

Gay little gamins along the street,
Dodging across under horses' feet,
A copper for drink or sore back to beat.

Children clad in velvet and lace
Envy you, pressing each eager face
To their windows, as scattering the mud you race.

Wingless sparrows and, like them, brown,
Bullied, then bullying—when ye are grown,
What is the outcome? Make it known.

Brothers, gather these waifs of the street,
Wash off their mudstains, make them meet,
With strengthened minds, our minds to greet.

'THE PATTER OF TINY FEET'

DEAR is the patter of tiny feet
Which falls on my ears with the morning light:
Tiny feet with their mighty clatter,
Tiny tongues with their ceaseless chatter—
Musical touches—the world how bright!

. . . . . .

Past is the patter of tiny feet,
But my heart still hears, with each morning's light,
Tiny feet with their mighty clatter,
Tiny tongues with their ceaseless chatter—
Such muffled echoes—and day is night!

ILLUSIONS PERDUES

I THOUGHT that I would dwell with love
    And love with me, till, ah ! one day
I found that he could faithless prove—
    He spread his wings and flew away.

I thought that I would sing for fame ;
    I stretched my hands to grasp the wreath,
Which in my eager clutch became
    Sere leaflets, withered by a breath.

I thought that I would gather wealth,
    To clothe and educate the poor,
To reach unto the stricken, health—
    'Twas dust that strewed my garner-floor.

I think that when I die, my soul
    Will melt into another land
Of all things perfected—the goal
    Of what we cannot understand.

And yet, perchance, I may but go
    Six feet, no further, merged in clay,
To be the food of flowers—and so
    My last illusion will decay.

www.ingramcontent.com/pod-product-compliance
Lightning Source LLC
Chambersburg PA
CBHW031120160426
43192CB00008B/1056